CGP

New CLAIT

Unit 4

Spreadsheets

The Course Book

CGP's Course Books offer a step-by-step approach
to help you really get to grips with New CLAIT.

Each topic is explained using everyday language,
with plenty of worked examples, handy hints and practical tasks.

Exactly what you need —
perfect for even the most 'computer-phobic' learners.

CONTENTS

Published by Coordination Group Publications Ltd.

Contributors:
Jo Anson
Charley Darbishire
Dominic Hall
Simon Little
Kate Redmond
Rachel Selway
Jennifer Underwood

Endorsed by OCR for use with OCR Level 1 Certificate for IT users - New CLAIT specification.

With thanks to Julie Forsdick and Kate Houghton for the proof-reading.

ISBN   1 84146 326 4

Groovy website: www.cgpbooks.co.uk
Jolly bits of clipart from CorelDRAW
Printed by Elanders Hindson, Newcastle upon Tyne.

With thanks to Microsoft for permission to use screenshots from
MS Excel and MS Windows XP.

What is New CLAIT?

This page will tell you a bit about the book and how to use it.

New CLAIT is a Computer Course for Beginners

In New CLAIT, you'll learn how to make computers work for you, so you can use things like:

- word processors — to write letters
- spreadsheets — to do your household accounts
- databases — to organise information
- e-mail — to keep in touch with people all over the world

Just Have a Go, You Won't Break it

The key to learning about computers is to try things.
Don't be afraid of it — you won't break the computer with a mouse and keyboard.
You'd need to open it up and pour a cup of tea inside to break it.

This book will take you through everything
step-by-step. You'll be doing things all the time.

When you've got to do things,
you'll find numbered shapes like this.

There are also practice exercises at the end of each section,
so you can see how you'd do in a real New CLAIT test.

Read this bit if you are a Tutor

1) We've used Microsoft Office XP and Microsoft Windows XP Professional
   for this book, but most things will be the same for older versions.

2) To keep things simple we've concentrated on one way of doing things instead
   of confusing people with five different ways to do the same thing.

3) There is a CD which accompanies this series of books. It contains all the files the student
   will need for the worked examples, practice exercises and exams. It also contains sample
   answer files for most of the exercises. The files have been saved in Excel 95 format for
   maximum compatibility.

This book has all you need to pass...

This book covers everything you need to know for New CLAIT Unit 4. So just sit back and enjoy
the next 38 pages. Well, don't sit back too far — you won't be able to reach the keyboard.

The Bits of a Computer

If you're learning about spreadsheets now, you must have some idea of what a computer looks like and which bits do what... But here's a wee reminder anyway, just in case.

The Parts of a Computer Do Different Jobs

Here's a computer — and all the bits are labelled.

Monitor — looks like a TV screen. What you're working on is displayed on it.

System box — the 'brain' of the computer, where all the bits and pieces that make it work can be found. You put CDs and disks in here, and plug all the other computer parts into the back.

Printer — used to make a paper copy of what's on your screen, like letters or photos.

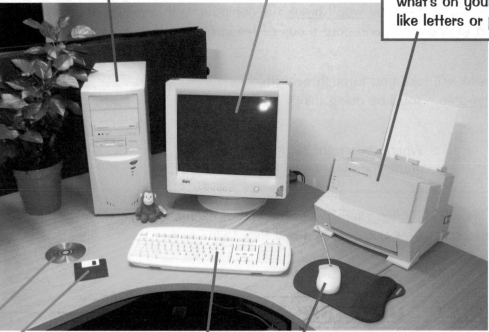

CDs and floppy disks — can be used to store your work. You can put them into a different computer and your work will appear.

Mouse — when you move this over your desk, a little arrow on the screen will move too. You can use it to select and change different things on the screen.

Keyboard — has keys with letters and numbers on that you press to enter information, e.g. to write a letter.

Thank you, but I know what a keyboard is...

If you feel like your intelligence is being insulted, you're allowed to skip to section 2... But I'd advise reading this first section — you never know what new things you might learn.

The Bits of a Computer

Here's another page of useful background information (slightly harder than the last page)...

Computers come in Different Shapes

Laptops are handy little computers that you can fold up, carry about in a bag and use on the train, should you fancy. They're as good as normal computers, just smaller.

Notebooks are like laptops, but smaller and a bit less powerful. (Still plenty good enough for us normal folks though.)

Computers are made of Hardware and Software

HARDWARE is all the physical bits of a computer — not just the obvious bits like the monitor, keyboard and printer, but also the gubbins inside that make it work.

SOFTWARE is all the programs in a computer that make it do different things — i.e. the instructions that tell the computer what to do. You can buy new software on CDs.

For example, 'Microsoft Word' is a program which lets you write letters and things. A computer game is another program, where the keys you press might guide a character round a special world. Nice.

Here are Some Terms You'll Need to Know

1) Programs, like 'Microsoft Word' or 'Microsoft Excel', are called applications.

2) Files are made with applications. They contain the things you make — a file from a word processor, like 'Microsoft Word', will be lots of text, and a file from a drawing program will be a picture.

3) A folder is a place where you can store files or applications. They're really useful for organising your computer.

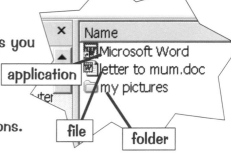

'Microsoft Windows' is a special program called an 'operating system' — it lets you interact with the computer, open and close other programs, and generally control what's going on — useful.

Programs like 'Microsoft Windows' let you do loads of things without having to understand what's really going on.

When you save, the computer stores your work as a file...

Files and folders in particular can be quite confusing at first. Remember — a folder is just a place to store files or more folders. They'll make more sense as you use them more.

4

Using the Keyboard

Before we get stuck into spreadsheets, it's a good idea to check you know some basics.

All Keyboards Look the Same (More or Less)

The big bit with the letters on is always the same — it's the same arrangement as on a typewriter. So if you've used a typewriter before, you should pick it up really easily.

Don't worry about these keys. They're called <u>function keys</u> and do special things in different programs.

These are <u>navigation keys</u>, and do things like taking you to the start or end of your work. Don't worry about most of these — you won't use many apart from '<u>Delete</u>'.

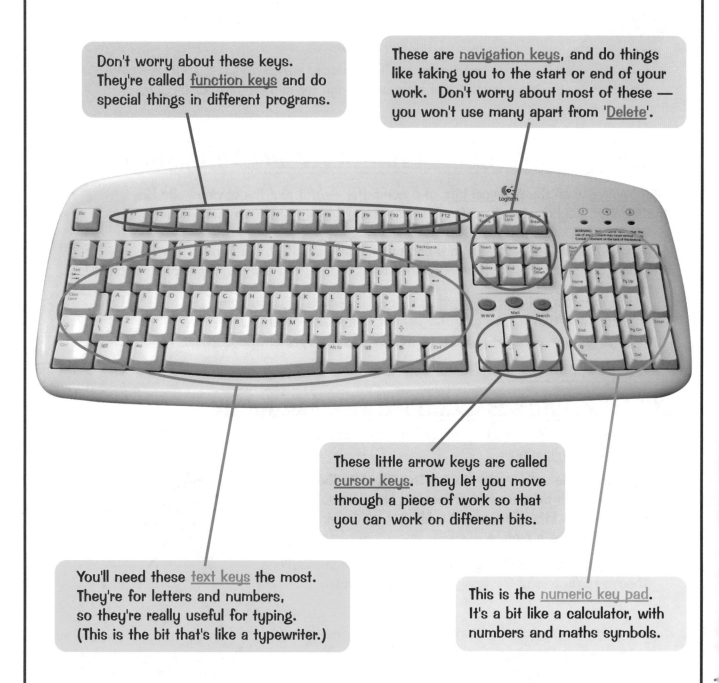

These little arrow keys are called <u>cursor keys</u>. They let you move through a piece of work so that you can work on different bits.

You'll need these <u>text keys</u> the most. They're for letters and numbers, so they're really useful for typing. (This is the bit that's like a typewriter.)

This is the <u>numeric key pad</u>. It's a bit like a calculator, with numbers and maths symbols.

This type of keyboard shouldn't play music...

If your keyboard has only two rows of keys — a bottom row of white keys and a top row of black keys arranged in groups of 2 and 3 (and is made by Casio, probably), then you have the wrong type of keyboard. That type is for creating sweet music, not typing. (An easy mistake).

Section One — Introduction

Using the Keyboard

And some more bits of the keyboard...

Some Keys are Really Special

Here's some of the keys you'll find really useful when you're typing:

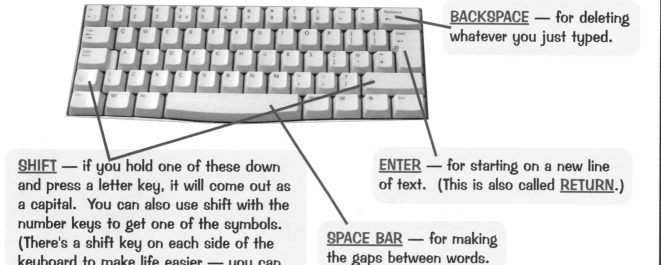

BACKSPACE — for deleting whatever you just typed.

ENTER — for starting on a new line of text. (This is also called RETURN.)

SPACE BAR — for making the gaps between words.

SHIFT — if you hold one of these down and press a letter key, it will come out as a capital. You can also use shift with the number keys to get one of the symbols. (There's a shift key on each side of the keyboard to make life easier — you can use either of them.)

Have a Go at Using the Keyboard

Learning to type is really slow to begin with, but you'll soon get better with practice. If you need a bit more practice, have a look at New Clait Unit 1 — Using a Computer.

 Open a word-processing application and have a go at typing:

- Make sure you're typing accurately. It doesn't matter if you're slow.
- You don't have to whack the keys — find out how lightly you can press a key to still make it work.
- Make sure you know how to use the four special keys above.

Your typing will get faster with time...

Don't worry, you'll soon be learning about spreadsheets, which is obviously why you're reading this book... Just checking you can do the easy bits before starting on the spreadsheety bits.

Get Used to the Mouse

These final two pages before we start spreadsheets will check that you're happy using a mouse.

First, Catch Your Mouse...

This is a mouse.

This is its left button.

This is its right button
(which you won't need for now).

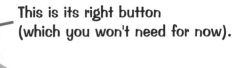

This is a mouse mat.

The mouse has a nice rounded top that you put your palm on,
and a couple of buttons at the top where your fingers go. Like this:

...Then Push it Around a bit

1) To use your mouse, all you have to do is push it around on your desk.
(You'll find that it glides along nicely on top of a foamy mouse mat.)

2) Underneath the mouse will be a little ball or a little red light.
This bit tells the computer how you are moving the mouse.

3) As you move the mouse, a little arrow on your screen
moves about. This arrow is called a pointer.

Pointers look a bit like this.
(But they're about ten times tinier.)

When you're using writing software, like 'Microsoft
Word', your pointer will look like this, but a lot smaller.

Don't worry if your pointer looks different to the ones above. It'll be really obvious —
the pointer is the thing that moves about on your screen when you move the mouse.

Try not to leave the ~~tail~~ wire dangling off the desk...

And this is another page of stuff you might feel you know already. Well don't worry, it's nearly
time to get on with spreadsheets. And then you'll wish you were back on a page about mice...

Get Used to the Mouse

And now, following on from how to spot a mouse, how to use it properly.

You'll need to use the Left Mouse Button all the time

You normally just 'click' the mouse button — give it a quick press
and then take your finger off again — you'll hear a little clicking noise.

- The left mouse button can 'select' things. This means that when you move the pointer
  over something and click your left mouse button, you'll make it 'alive' and useable.

- If you 'double-click' the left mouse button — quickly click on something twice —
  you'll be able to open programs and make things work.

Try this Quick Activity for Learning Mouse Control

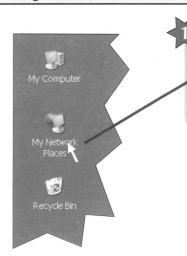

 1 Move the mouse around until the pointer on the screen is on top of an icon. (An icon is a little picture, representing a file or application.)

2 Click the left mouse button once. The icon will get darker — become highlighted. This means you have selected it.

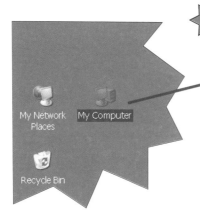

 3 Move the pointer over a different icon. Press the left mouse button down and keep it held down. Then move your mouse and you'll find you can drag the icon about. Useful.

4 If you 'double-click' on an icon (move your pointer to it and do a quick 'click click'), you'll make it open.

Click click, bom bom, bop shoo wop shoo wop...

This does sound a bit confusing on paper, but once you've had a go at the clicking, you'll be fine.
What you've got to remember is — left once selects, left twice opens, left-hold-move drags.

Spreadsheet Basics

Spreadsheets are really useful for organising information and doing calculations.

You Can Open Excel Through 'Start'

The spreadsheet software you'll find on your computer is probably 'Microsoft Excel'. Others exist, like Lotus 1-2-3 and the spreadsheet in Microsoft Works, but Excel is the most common.

You can open 'Microsoft Excel' the same way as most other programs — through the 'Start' menu.

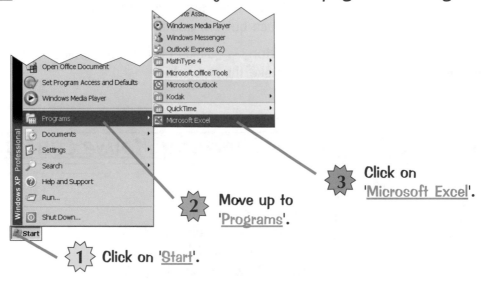

3 Click on 'Microsoft Excel'.

2 Move up to 'Programs'.

1 Click on 'Start'.

Spreadsheets are Useful for Budgets

Here's a demonstration of how useful spreadsheets are:

You're having a party and you have £50 to spend, but can't work out exactly how to spend the money.

You could work it all out by hand, but it's annoying, time-consuming and messy.

4 ~~5~~ bottles of wine (£3.50 each):   ~~£17.50~~ £14.00
1 crate of beer (£15 each):   £15.00
2 ~~3~~ bottles of lemonade (60p each):   ~~£1.80~~ £1.20
3 ~~2~~ bottles of coke (60p each):   ~~£1.20~~ £1.80
2 fancy cakes (£3 each):   £6.00
3 ~~4~~ family packs of crisps (£2 each):   ~~£8.00~~ £6.00
4 packs of sausage rolls (50p each):   £2.00
2 ~~3~~ packet of balloons (70p each):   ~~10p~~ £1.40
1 tape of cheesy party music   £2.50
                    ~~£54.10~~ £49.90

	A	B	C	D
1	Party budget			
2				
3	item	cost (£)	no.	total cost (£)
4	wine	3.5	4	14
5	beer	15	1	15
6	lemonade	0.6	2	1.2
7	coke	0.6	3	1.8
8	cake	3	2	6
9	crisps	2	3	6
10	sausage rolls	0.5	4	2
11	balloons	0.7	2	1.4
12	music	2.5	1	2.5
13				
14			grand total	49.9

It would be much simpler to use a spreadsheet. Once you've filled it in, you can fiddle with the number of items, or their cost, and your total cost will automatically update itself.

Don't bodge it when you budget — use spreadsheets...

Once you get the hang of it, you'll find it's much easier to use a spreadsheet than to work things out by hand. The spreadsheet does all the work for you, and then even updates itself. Wow.

Spreadsheet Basics

It's important to get to know the basic layout of a spreadsheet before you try to use it.

Spreadsheets are Just Loads of Cells

A spreadsheet has loads of boxes arranged in rows and columns. Each box is called a cell.

Here's an empty spreadsheet:

This is the formula bar. When you click on a cell, its contents will appear here and you can edit it.

Cells are named using letters and numbers...

...so this is cell A6...

...and this is cell B8.

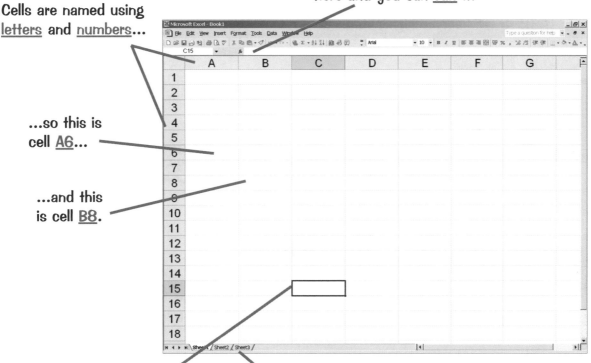

This cell has been selected. If you type something, it will appear here.

'Microsoft Excel' calls each file of spreadsheets a workbook. Each workbook can contain lots of different worksheets (spreadsheet pages like this one). Click on these tabs to go to different worksheets within a workbook.

Use the cursor keys to move from cell to cell. Or just click on a cell with the mouse.

Spreadsheets are so exciting I could just explode...

OK, that's maybe getting carried away a little. But spreadsheets are certainly very useful for a multitude of different tasks. Soon, you'll be wondering how you ever managed without them.

Changing Data in Cells

You're not going to get very far with spreadsheets if you can't enter data...

To Enter Data Just Click and Type

Here's how to <u>enter</u> data in a spreadsheet:

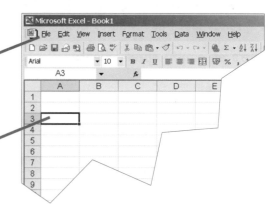

1 <u>Create</u> a new spreadsheet by <u>clicking</u> on '<u>File</u>' and then on '<u>New</u>' (or you can just use the new blank spreadsheet that pops up automatically when you open Excel).

2 Click on the <u>cell</u> you want to enter data in (**A3**). It will become highlighted.

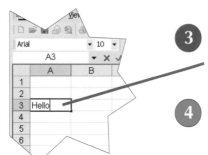

3 Just <u>type</u>. Your writing will automatically appear in the <u>cell</u>. Press <u>Enter</u> when you've finished.

4 Move to cell **B2** with the <u>cursor</u> keys, or click on it with the <u>mouse</u>. Then just <u>type</u>, like before. Easy.

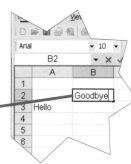

You Can Delete Data if You Like

<u>Deleting</u> data's not hard either:

 Open the file '<u>random numbers</u>'.

This file can be found on the accompanying CD. Ask your tutor to help you find it.

To delete the <u>whole contents</u> of a cell:

 <u>Click</u> on cell A7 to <u>select</u> it.

 Press the <u>delete</u> key.

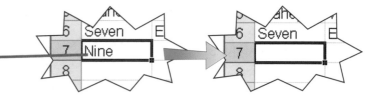

To delete the contents of <u>lots of cells</u>:

 <u>Click</u> on cell A1. Check that your pointer looks like a white cross and <u>hold</u> the mouse button down.

 <u>Drag</u> your mouse until all the cells you want to delete are <u>highlighted</u>.

 Press the <u>delete</u> key.

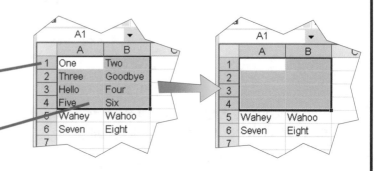

Click and type again — it's not brain surgery...

When you've entered data in a cell, you'd normally press Enter which drops you to the cell below. You can also press the Tab key (above "Caps Lock") to jump you to the next cell along.

Changing Data in Cells

And the excitement continues with... amending data in a spreadsheet.

You Can Correct Your Mistakes

It's easy to make mistakes entering data — everyone does it. You don't want to delete the whole cell and retype it — it makes more sense to just correct the mistake itself, like so:

1 Open the spreadsheet 'Winter Olympics2'.

2 Spot your mistake. There's one here.

3 Click on the cell with the mistake in.

The contents of the cell will appear in the formula bar.

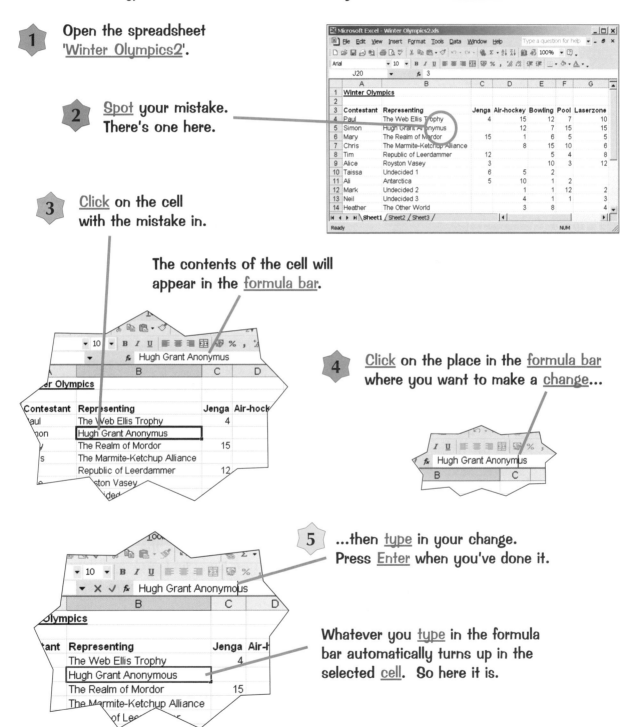

4 Click on the place in the formula bar where you want to make a change...

5 ...then type in your change. Press Enter when you've done it.

Whatever you type in the formula bar automatically turns up in the selected cell. So here it is.

Just try not to make mistakes in the first place...

Bet you're getting a bit bored now — I know I am. *Yawn* Anyway, find them thrilling, or find yourself falling asleep, it's important that you have a go. So off you go — edit stuff. *Yawn*

Rows and Columns

Rows and columns are, well, things that go across and things that go up and down.
But I'm sure you know that already. Here's a bit about the rows and columns on spreadsheets.

Rows and Columns are Easy to Spot

You can recognise rows and columns
already I expect, but just in case...

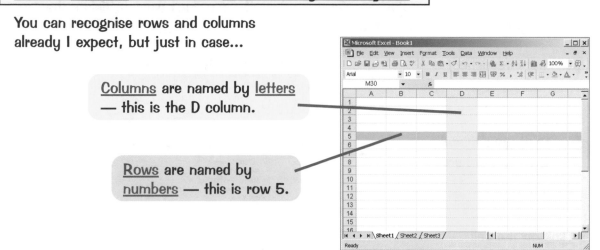

Columns are named by letters
— this is the D column.

Rows are named by
numbers — this is row 5.

Rows and Columns can be Adjusted

Often you'll find that what you type doesn't quite fit in its column,
and gets covered up by the next cell along. Well, never fear — just do this:

1 Open the spreadsheet
'People and computers'.

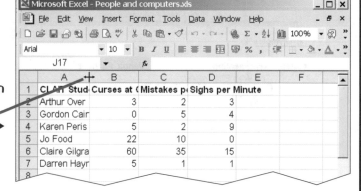

2 Move your pointer between the column
headings, A and B. It should
turn into a double-arrow like this: ⟷

3 Double-click and your column
will become the perfect size.

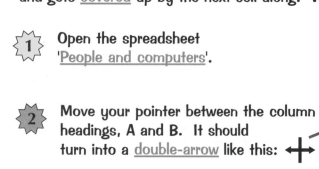

Ahh. That's better.

4 You can make the column any size
you like. Just click and drag the
double-arrow 'til you're happy.

You can do the same with rows —
move your pointer to the line between
two row numbers and you'll get a
double-arrow like before. Amazing.

But beware — printers can mess up your plans...

When you're printing spreadsheets, you'll find that different printers often give different results
— sometimes your data will fit in the column, and sometimes it won't. You'll soon get to know
your printer, but you might find it helpful to make your columns slightly extra-wide, just in case.

Rows and Columns

Imagine you've made a spreadsheet. Feel proud for a second. But wait — isn't there a column missing from the middle? Oh no, should you delete it all and start again? Nope, course not...

Sometimes You Might Need Extra Rows or Columns...

The spreadsheet 'People and computers' is missing a column which needs to go between columns A and B. To add a new column just do this:

 1 You want to add a new column to the left of column B. Select column B by clicking on the letter at the top.

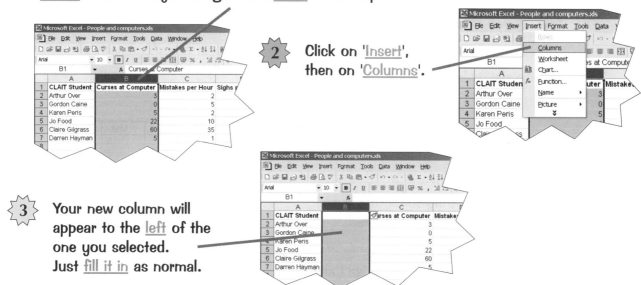

2 Click on 'Insert', then on 'Columns'.

3 Your new column will appear to the left of the one you selected. Just fill it in as normal.

It's just as easy to insert new rows. Select a row (by clicking on the row's number.) Click on 'Insert' and then on 'Rows'. Hey presto — a new row will be inserted above your selected row.

...and Sometimes You Might Want to Delete Them

1 Select the new column B by clicking on its letter.

2 Click on 'Edit', then on 'Delete', and wave goodbye to that column.

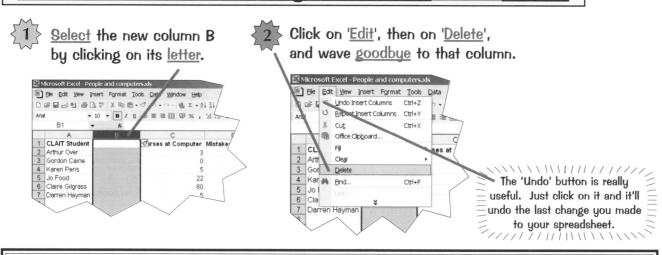

The 'Undo' button is really useful. Just click on it and it'll undo the last change you made to your spreadsheet.

Don't get 'delete' confused with 'insert'...

You can delete individual cells too, by selecting them and clicking on 'Edit', then 'Delete'. But don't do this if you really mean to delete a row or column — it's the best way to mess up.

Deleting, Hiding and Clearing Data

There are three different ways of making data disappear — deleting, hiding and clearing.

Deleting Removes Data, Not Formats

You already know how to <u>delete</u> the data in a cell (see page 10),
but here's a demo of why it's not always so great:

 Open the file '<u>CLAIT exam marks</u>'.

 <u>Select</u> the cells you want to <u>delete</u> by
clicking and dragging (see page 10).

	A	B	C
1	CLAIT exam marks		
2	First name	Last name	Unit 1
3	Theresa	Green	100
4	Ben	Dover	56
5	Tanya	Hide	98
	Arth	Brain	

 Press the <u>delete</u> key.

 <u>Type</u> some <u>new text</u> in
the now blank cells.

	A	B	C
1	new text		
2	new text	new text	Unit 1
3	new text	new text	100
4	new text	new text	56
5	Tanya	Hide	98
	Arth	Brain	

You'll notice how the cells stay <u>formatted</u> even
though their original contents were deleted.

So, where the original text was <u>bold</u>, or <u>bordered</u> or in a <u>coloured cell</u>,
the new text will be the same... which isn't always how you want it.

You'll be learning to format cells on page 29.

Clearing Removes Data And Formats

 <u>Select</u> the cells you want to <u>clear</u> by
clicking and dragging (see page 10).

	A	B	C
1	new text		
2	new text	new text	Unit 1
3	new text	new text	100
4	new text	new text	56
5	Tanya	Hide	98
	Arth	Brain	

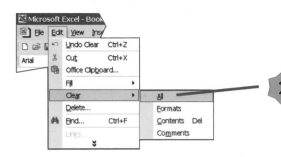

 Click on '<u>Edit</u>', then go down to
'<u>Clear</u>', and across to click on '<u>All</u>'.

 <u>Type</u> some <u>new text</u> in the blank cells.
You'll notice that your new text is <u>normal</u> —
<u>not</u> bold or bordered or in a coloured cell.

	A	B	C
1	Practice exams		
2	First name	Surname	Unit 1
3	Jenny	Underwood	100
4	Rachel	Selway	56
5	Tanya	Hide	98
	Arth	Brain	

Clearing saves a lot of time, believe me...

It's amazing how useful clearing is. Before I heard about clearing, I'd spend a lot of time
un-bolding, un-colouring and un-bordering every cell I wanted to be blank. I'm an idiot.

Deleting, Hiding and Clearing Data

Hiding's a nifty little trick. It's not hard to do, and it'll make you look like a real pro.

You Can Hide Rows and Columns

When you start using spreadsheets for really huge complicated calculations, you'll find it makes sense to hide the boring calculation bits. Then your spreadsheet only displays the interesting results. It's different to deleting — your hidden data isn't gone, you just can't see it, and you can unhide it again if you want to.

To hide a row or column, all you do is:

1 Select the row or column you want to hide by clicking on its number or letter at the edge of the spreadsheet.

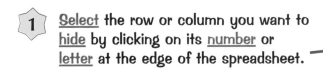

2 Click on 'Format', then go down to 'Row' (or 'Column', depending on what you've selected), and across to click on 'Hide'.

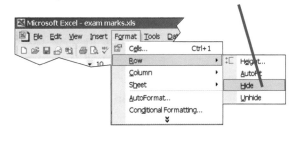

3 The row or column you selected will disappear... as if by magic.

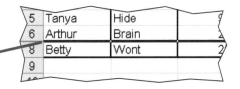

You Can Unhide Them Too

1 Select the rows (or columns) either side of the hidden one.

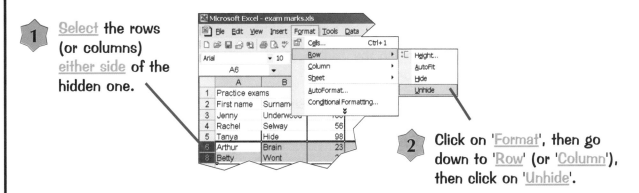

2 Click on 'Format', then go down to 'Row' (or 'Column'), then click on 'Unhide'.

Hey presto — your hidden row or column will magically reappear.

Hey, you've got to hide your cells away...

...so sang John Lennon (I think). Don't worry too much about "Hide" — it's not something you'll need to do a lot. It can be really handy sometimes though, so remember that it's there...

Saving and Closing

So now you've had a play and made a few spreadsheets... but how do you save and close?

Saving Means You Won't Lose Your Work

1 <u>Create</u> a new spreadsheet and <u>type</u> your address in the first column.

2 <u>Save</u> your document by clicking on '<u>Save As</u>' in the '<u>File</u>' menu.

You'll get a new window like this:

Always use 'Save As' when you want to give a file a name, or save it in a different folder. Only use 'Save' when you want to save changes to the same file.

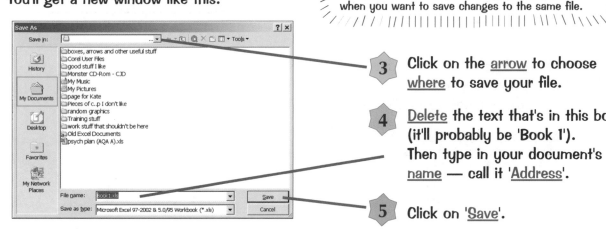

3 Click on the <u>arrow</u> to choose <u>where</u> to save your file.

4 <u>Delete</u> the text that's in this box (it'll probably be 'Book 1'). Then type in your document's <u>name</u> — call it '<u>Address</u>'.

5 Click on '<u>Save</u>'.

Save Another Version of Your Work

1 Save a <u>second version</u> of your file — click on '<u>Save As</u>' in the 'File' menu.

2 Now repeat steps 2 to 4 from above, but name your document '<u>Address 2</u>'.

Close Your File When You're Finished

1 <u>Close</u> 'Address 2' by clicking '<u>Close</u>' in the 'File' menu.

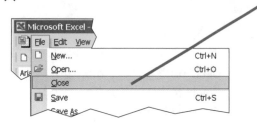

If you don't <u>save</u> before you close, you'll get a message like this:

2 Click on '<u>Yes</u>' to save, or '<u>No</u>' just to close without saving.

"Save" yourself from doing it again...

You're probably fed up with all that clicking — but it's worth learning the basic stuff properly, so you don't have problems when it gets trickier later on. You know it makes sense...

Printing

Printing... Aah, that thing where paper comes out of a machine with words and stuff on. Got it.

You Can Print **Your Spreadsheet**

1 Click on 'File', then 'Print'.

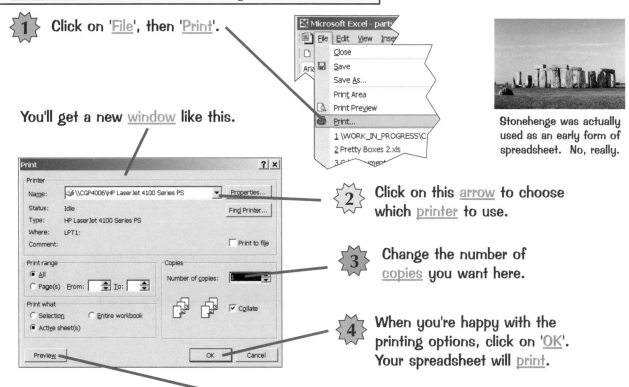

Stonehenge was actually used as an early form of spreadsheet. No, really.

You'll get a new window like this.

2 Click on this arrow to choose which printer to use.

3 Change the number of copies you want here.

4 When you're happy with the printing options, click on 'OK'. Your spreadsheet will print.

It's a good idea to click on 'Preview' before you click on 'OK'. This will give you a print preview, which lets you see what your print-out will look like before you print.

You Can Print **Formulas Too**

Formulas — what are they? They're what the next section is all about — see P20 onwards.

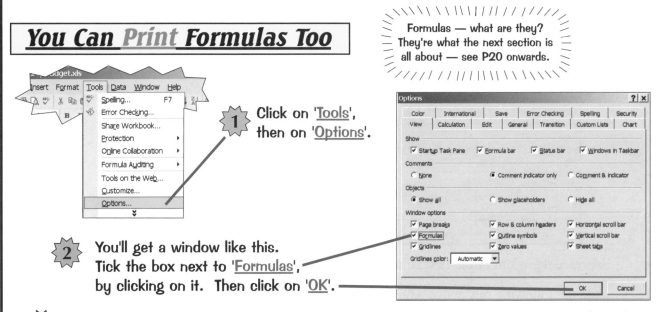

1 Click on 'Tools', then on 'Options'.

2 You'll get a window like this. Tick the box next to 'Formulas', by clicking on it. Then click on 'OK'.

3 Repeat steps 1 to 4 above, and you'll get another printout, this time with your formulas printed. (To go back to normal, just do the same but this time untick the 'Formulas' box.)

And for my final trick...

If you only want to print part of a spreadsheet — just select the cells you want to print first. Then, in the print menu, click on the 'Selection' button (just below 'Print what'). Ta da...

Section Two — Practice Exercises

Before moving on to the next section, try these exercises to see how much you've learnt so far.

Exercise 1

1. Open Excel.

2. Create a new spreadsheet.

3. Enter this data into the spreadsheet:

Facility	Jan	Feb	Mar
Swimming Pool	768	659	689
Sun Booth	56	42	78
Gym	579	605	436
Bike Spinning	354	265	145

4. Increase the width of the first column to ensure that all data is displayed in full.

5. Add the following row above **Gym**:

Squash	68	87	55

6. Delete the row for **Sun Booth**.

7. Insert a new column named **Price** between **Facility** and **Jan**.

8. Check your data and then save the spreadsheet as **Leisure Centre**.

9. When you have finished, close the file.

Exercise 2

1. Create a new spreadsheet.

2. Enter this data into the spreadsheet:

Item	Sep	Oct	Nov
Crisps	45	67	36
Milk	45	37	56
Apples	49	55	64
Bananas	34	56	88
Twix	108	89	124

3. Increase the width of the first column to ensure that all data is displayed in full.

4. Add the following row above **Apples**:

Fruit Bars	68	87	55

5. Insert a new column named **Price** between **Item** and **Sep**.

6. Delete the row for **Milk**.

7. Check your data and then save the spreadsheet as **Tuck Shop**.

8. When you have finished, close the file.

Section Two — Practice Exercises

Here are some more exercises. It's not that bad, this spreadsheet lark. Just hang in there.

Exercise 3

1.   Create a new spreadsheet.

2.   Enter this data into the spreadsheet:

Module Database Design			
Student Names	Assignment 1	Assignment 2	Exam
Anderson D	45	56	45
Sherwood P	78	76	63
Patel M	78	83	71
Holling W	24	35	32
Mendez L	47	58	52

3.   Delete the row for **Sherwood P**.

4.   Add the following row above **Mendez L**:

Jones P	68	87	55

5.   Insert a new column named **Coursework** between **Assignment 2** and **Exam**.

6.   Increase the width of all the columns to ensure that all data is displayed in full.

7.   Check your data and then save the spreadsheet as **Results**.

8.   When you have finished, close the file.

Exercise 4

1.   Create a new spreadsheet.

2.   Enter this data into the spreadsheet:

Sales for March						
Agent	Base Pay	Rate	Week 1	Week 2	Week 3	Week 4
Sally	18	0.15	22	35	12	16
Navinder	22	0.16	23	35	35	22
James	14	0.22	8	7	6	9
Famia	25	0.15	28	31	34	22
Sue	15	0.16	23	18	17	14

3.   Add the following row above **Navinder**:

Hassan	18	0.22	18	14	15	16

4.   Delete the row for **Sally**.

5.   Increase the width of the columns to ensure that all data is displayed in full.

6.   Check your data and then save the spreadsheet as **Agent Sales**.

7.   When you have finished, close the file.

Simple Formulas

Without formulas, spreadsheets are just fancy tables.
It's the formulas that make them so amazingly useful.

A Formula is just a Calculation

Formulas do stuff like <u>adding up</u> for you.
The four main signs you'll need are:

| + (add) | - (subtract) | * (multiply) | / (divide) |

Here's how to use a formula to <u>calculate</u> the total number of
curries eaten by a contestant in the curry eating championships:

 1 Open the '<u>Microsoft Excel</u>' document '<u>Curry Championships</u>'.

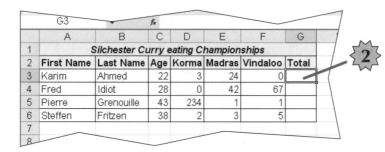

2 Click your mouse in cell <u>G3</u>.

3 Type an '<u>equals sign</u>' (=).
This shows the computer
that you're going to enter
a <u>formula</u>.

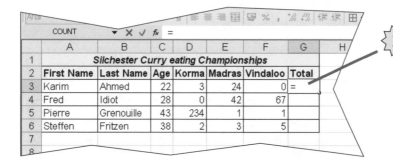

 4 Now click with your mouse on the <u>first cell</u> you want to add up — that's <u>D3</u>.

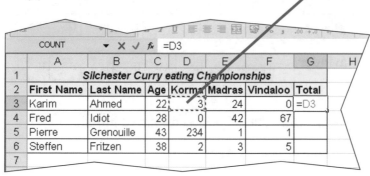

Simple Formulas

Just Type the Sum into the Cell

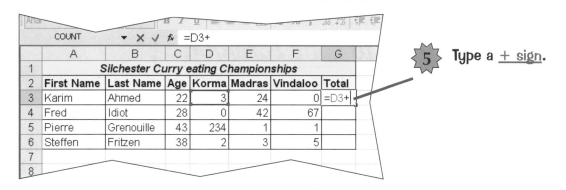

5 Type a + sign.

6 Now click on cell **E3**, type another + sign, then click on cell **F3**.

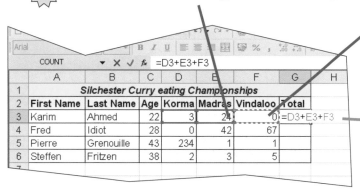

You should have the sum
=D3+E3+F3.

7 Press the 'Enter' key to finish the formula.

Now the cell shows the
answer to the sum:
3+24+0=27.

You may also need to use brackets ( ) in your formulas, for
example if you want to add two cells together before you
multiply them: e.g. **5+4*3=17**
but with brackets: **(5+4)*3=27**

Trisha moved the mouse quietly,
allowing Bev to believe that her
pen was controlling the computer.

I can't see the formula any more...

You'll notice that once you've completed the formula, the cell just shows the answer to the
calculation. To see exactly what it's calculating, click on the cell and look at the formula bar.

Copying Formulas

Once you've typed a formula once, you can copy it to save you typing it out again.
This saves loads of time, which comes in handy for painting your nails, or other useful things.

You can _Click_ and _Drag_ to _Copy Formulas_

 Open the 'Microsoft Excel' document 'Sweet Shop'.

	COUNT ▼ X ✓ fx	=B3*C3			
	A	B	C	D	E
1		Sweet Sales			
2	Type of sweet	Price per packet	Packets sold	Total sales	
3	Mint Gumboils	£0.50	250	=B3*C3	
4	Candied Turnips	£0.75	25		
5	Kipper Pastilles	£0.15	500		
6	Chocolate Lice	£0.48	10		
7					

2 Click on cell D3 to select it. Type an equals sign in it (=).

Click on cell B3, type the multiplication sign (*), then click on cell C3.

Press the 'Enter' key.

Now your spreadsheet should look like this.

The formula in D3 multiplies B3 by C3 to calculate the total sales value of Mint Gumboils.

		fx		
	A	B	C	D
1		Sweet Sales		
2	Type of sweet	Price per packet	Packets sold	Total sales
3	Mint Gumboils	£0.50	250	£125.00
4	Candied Turnips	£0.75	25	
5	Kipper Pastilles	£0.15	500	
6	Chocolate Lice	£0.48	10	
7				

If you want to find out the total sales value for the other rows in your spreadsheet, you could type the formulas out one by one. But a much easier way is to copy the formula you created in D3...

 Click on the cell D3, which contains the formula you want to copy.

	D3	fx	=B3*C3		
	A	B	C	D	E
1		Sweet Sales			
2	Type of sweet	Price per packet	Packets sold	Total sales	
3	Mint Gumboils	£0.50	250	£125.00	
4	Candied Turnips	£0.75	25		
5	Kipper Pastilles	£0.15	500		
6	Chocolate Lice	£0.48	10		
7					
8					

4 Now move your mouse over the bottom right hand corner of the cell, until your pointer changes to a cross.

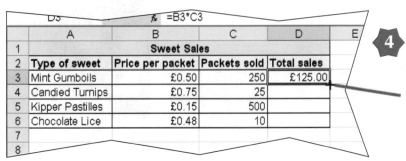

Your mouse pointer needs to change to look like this: ╋
It won't work if it looks like this ✚ or this ⟷ .

Copying Formulas

 Press the left mouse button, <u>hold it down</u>, and drag it down the column until D4, D5, and D6 are <u>highlighted</u>.

 Now <u>release</u> the mouse button. The formula will be copied to the cells you selected.

The original formula in D3 multiplied the two cells to the left of it, i.e. <u>B3</u> and <u>C3</u>.

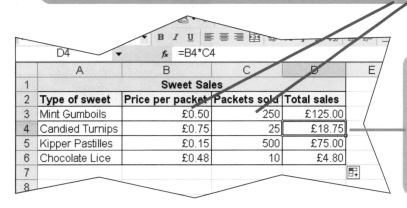

When you copy it to cell D4, it <u>changes</u> the cells it uses to calculate the formula, so D4 multiplies the two cells to the <u>left</u> of <u>it</u>, i.e. <u>B4</u> and <u>C4</u>. In the same way, D5 will multiply B5 by C5, and so on...

You can also Copy and Paste Formulas

This does exactly the same thing as clicking and dragging formulas.

 Click on the cell containing the formula you want to copy. Click on '<u>Edit</u>', then on '<u>Copy</u>'.

 Now select the cell (or cells) you want to paste it to, then click on 'Edit' again, then on '<u>Paste</u>'.

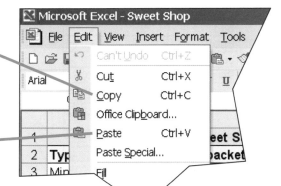

Wow...my computer's psychic...

It's weird how the computer knows to change the formula when you copy and paste it. If this wasn't what you wanted it to do, don't worry, you can always change it.

Automatic Updates

If you've used formulas in a spreadsheet, when you change things, the answers should change automatically to match your new data (but always check to make sure nothing's gone wrong).

If you *Change Data*, the Formulas will *Recalculate*

Let's say that you want to find out what will happen to the price of a cake if the price of one of the ingredients (chipmunks), increases to £10.

 1 Open the 'Microsoft Excel' document 'Cake Company'.

	A	B	C
1	Mrs Mingin's Lemon and Chipmunk Cake Company		
2	*Ingredient*	*Cost per 1kg cake*	
3	Flour	£0.20	
4	Eggs	£0.55	
5	Sugar	£0.50	
6	Butter	£0.80	
7	Lemons	£0.30	
8	Raisins	£0.70	
9	Chipmunks	£4.50	
10	Decorations	£0.43	
11			
12	Staff wages	£10.00	
13	Total Cost	£17.98	
14	Profit margin	20%	
15	Selling price	£21.58	
16			

 2 Click on cell B9, delete '4.50', and type '10' instead.

> This spreadsheet is formatted to show the £ sign. You'll learn how to do this on pages 32-33.

	A	B	C
1	Mrs Mingin's Lemon and Chipmunk Cake Company		
2	*Ingredient*	*Cost per 1kg cake*	
3	Flour	£0.20	
4	Eggs	£0.55	
5	Sugar	£0.50	
6	Butter	£0.80	
7	Lemons	£0.30	
8	Raisins	£0.70	
9	Chipmunks	£10.00	
10	Decorations	£0.43	
11			
12	Staff wages	£10.00	
13	Total Cost	£23.48	
14	Profit margin	20%	
15	Selling price	£28.18	
16			

 3 Now press 'Enter'.

> The formulas have automatically recalculated using the new data. You can see that the total cost of the cake has increased, and so has the selling price.

The answers change just like magic...except it's not...

This is a really useful feature. You could use it in your home accounts to see what would happen to your budget if your mortgage payments went up, or other fun things like that.

Adding up Lots of Numbers

There's an easy way to add up lots of numbers in your spreadsheets.

Use the Autosum Function to Add things up

 1 Open the 'Microsoft Excel' document 'Fantasy Football'.

 2 Click in cell C8 to select it.

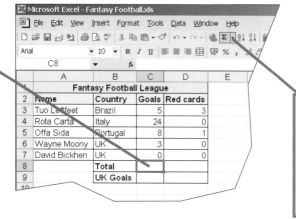

3 Now click on the 'Autosum' button.

The computer highlights the cells that it's going to add up.

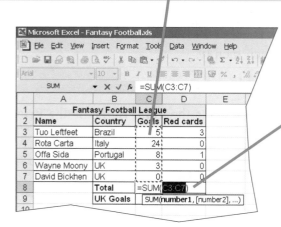

It also shows you the formula — SUM(C3:C7) means it will add up C3+C4+C5+C6+C7.

 4 These are the cells you want the computer to add up, so press 'Enter'.

Sometimes when you click on Autosum, the computer won't select the right cells for you.

If you want to add up different cells from the ones the computer selects:

Before you press enter (step 4 above) just click and drag with the mouse to select the ones you want.

You don't have to type it all in yourself...

You don't actually need to use autosum to pass the assessment, but it's so much quicker than writing a great big adding-up formula that it's really worth learning.

Section Three — Practice Exercises

Phew, that's another section finished. Now, get some practice done on this little lot.

Exercise 1

1.   Open 'Microsoft Excel'.

2.   Open the **Leisure Centre** spreadsheet.

3.   Enter this data for the **Price** column:

Price
2.5
3
2.6
1.8

4.   Add a new column named **Total**, after the **Mar** column.

5.   The total for each type of facility is calculated by adding the figures for Jan, Feb and Mar.

      Insert a formula to calculate the total for **Swimming Pool**.

      Replicate this formula to show the total for each facility.

6.   Add an extra column to the right of **Total** called **Income**.

7.   The income for each facility is calculated by multiplying the **Total** figure by the **Price**.

      Insert a formula to calculate the income for **Swimming Pool**.

      Replicate this formula to show the income for each facility.

8.   Add a new row after **Bike Spinning** entitled **Totals**.

9.   Enter formulas to calculate monthly totals for Jan, Feb and Mar.

10.   Check the data, then print out a copy of the spreadsheet.

11.   Save the spreadsheet as **Leisure2**, then close the file.

Section Three — Practice Exercises

Here's one more, just to make sure you've got the hang of it.

Exercise 2

1.   Open 'Microsoft Excel'.

2.   Open the **Tuck Shop** spreadsheet.

3.   Enter this data for the **Price** column into the spreadsheet:

Price
30
65
35
20
25

4.   Add a new column named **Total**, after the **Nov** column.

5.   The total for each type of item is calculated by adding the figures for Sep, Oct and Nov.

Insert a formula to calculate the total for **Crisps**.

Replicate this formula to show the total for each item.

6.   Add an extra column to the right of **Total** called **Income**.

7.   The income for each item is calculated by multiplying the **Total** figure by the **Price** and then dividing by 100.

Insert a formula to calculate the income for **Crisps**.

Replicate this formula to show the income for each item.

8.   Amend the figure for **Price** of **Bananas** to 22.

9.   Check the data, then print out a copy of the spreadsheet.

10.   Save the spreadsheet as **Tuck Shop2**, then close the file.

Aligning Cell Data

You can change the position of the data in a cell. It's called aligning.

You can Align to the Left , Right or Centre of a Cell

If you've done Unit 2 — Word Processing, then you'll
recognise the alignment buttons from 'Microsoft Word'.

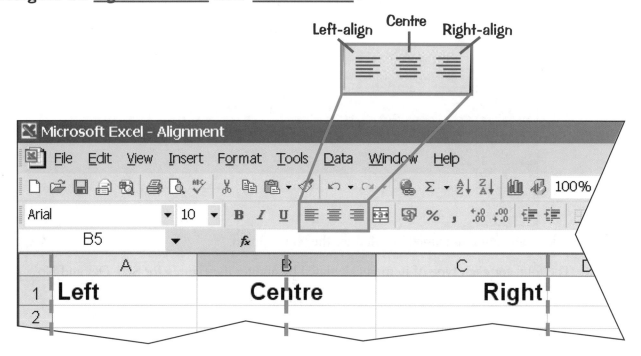

There are some Alignment Rules

The computer will automatically align spreadsheet data using certain rules:

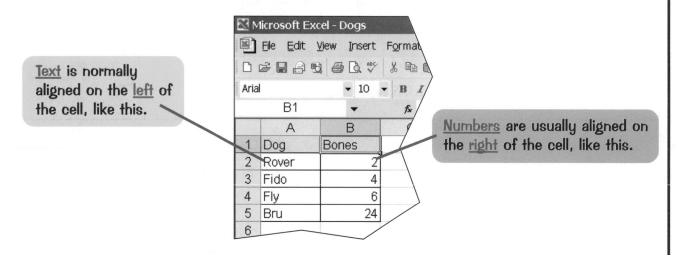

Text is normally aligned on the left of the cell, like this.

Numbers are usually aligned on the right of the cell, like this.

Left-right-left-right...

You can align things any way you want, really, but try to be consistent.
It can look good if you right-align the headings above columns of numbers.

Aligning Cell Data

You'll need to change the alignment of some data as part of your assessment.

It's Easy to Change the Alignment

 Open the 'Microsoft Excel' document 'Dogs'.

Click on cell B1 to select it.

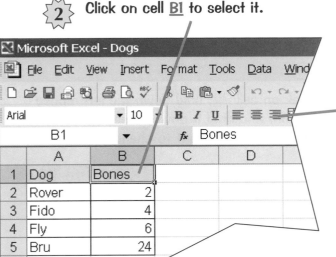

Now click the right-align button.

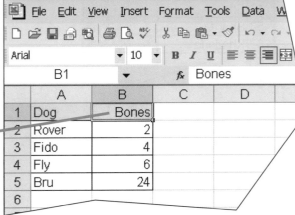

Hey presto — 'Bones' is now aligned on the right.

There are Loads More Types of Formatting...

Here are some other bits of formatting you can do to text and cells.
Select a cell then click on one of these buttons to see what happens:

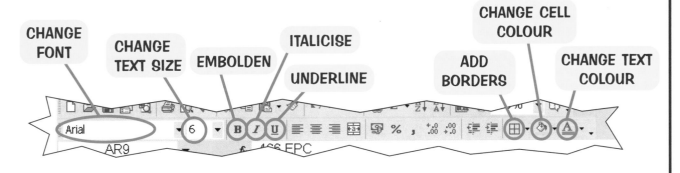

CHANGE FONT · CHANGE TEXT SIZE · EMBOLDEN · ITALICISE · UNDERLINE · ADD BORDERS · CHANGE CELL COLOUR · CHANGE TEXT COLOUR

I've got lots of things lined up...

For changing fonts, colours and borders, you can use the little arrows next to the buttons to select from a range of different options. Have a play with them and you'll see what I mean.

Formatting Numbers

You can change the way that numbers look in your spreadsheet — I bet you can hardly wait...

You can Change the Number of Decimal Places

 1 Open the 'Microsoft Excel' document '<u>Exam marks</u>'.

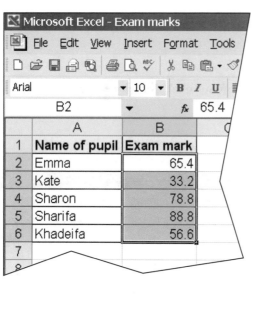

2 Click on cell <u>B2</u>, hold down the left mouse button, and drag it down to cell <u>B6</u> to select all the cells you want to change.

 3 Click on '<u>Format</u>', then on <u>Cells</u>.

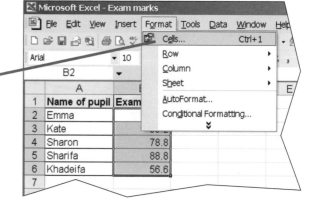

These bits (Number, Font, Border etc) are <u>tabs</u> — have a go at clicking on them to move to different pages.

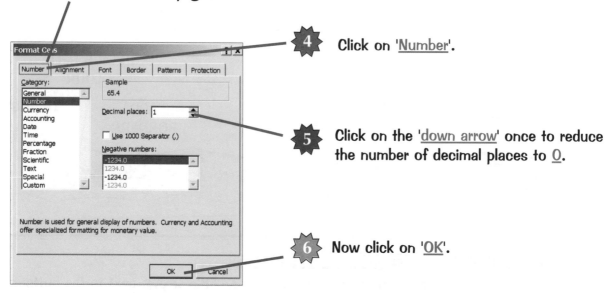

4 Click on '<u>Number</u>'.

5 Click on the '<u>down arrow</u>' once to reduce the number of decimal places to <u>0</u>.

6 Now click on '<u>OK</u>'.

Formatting Numbers

Now all the numbers are shown with no decimal places. This is called integer format.

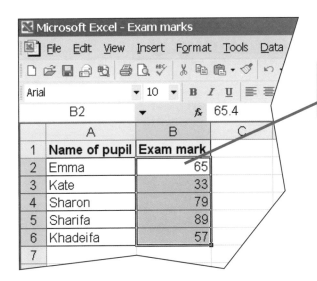

This box says 65. But click on it and you'll see 65.4 in the <u>formula bar</u> — which shows that your <u>original data</u> is still there.

Harold and Brenda spent hours in the jungle looking for integers.

A Formula uses your Original Data

If you write a <u>formula</u> that uses these cells, it will use the <u>real value</u> of the data, not the one that's showing after you formatted it — this can make some calculations look wrong.

 Create a <u>new</u> spreadsheet.

This sum seems <u>easy</u> enough: C2 will contain '= A2 + B2'.

 Enter this <u>data</u> and this <u>sum</u>.

	A	B	C
1	**A**	**B**	**Total**
2	2.6	2.7	5.3
3			

 <u>Format</u> your data to <u>no</u> decimal places.

 <u>Look</u> at what happens to your sum.

The contents of cells A2 and B2 are <u>still</u> 2.6 and 2.7, and the answer is 5.3, but they've all been rounded to the <u>nearest whole number</u>, which makes the sum look <u>wrong</u>.

Arial · 10 · **B** *I* <u>U</u>

C2 ▼ *fx* =SUM(A2:B2)

	A	B	C	D
1	**A**	**B**	**Total**	
2	3	3	5	
3				

So 3+3 equals 5 then...

Don't worry if this is a bit confusing at first. If the maths on your spreadsheet doesn't make sense, check the real values of the cells in the formula bar.

Section Four — Changing the Appearance

Formatting Numbers

If you've got prices or any kind of money in your spreadsheet, you need currency format.

Currency *is just* Another Kind *of* Formatting

1 Open the 'Microsoft Excel' document '<u>Activity Breaks</u>'.

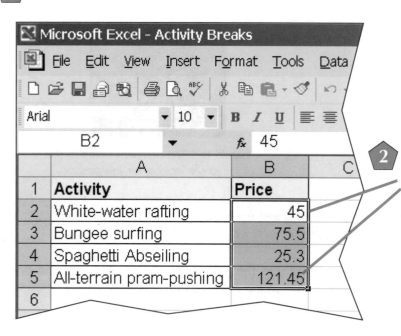

2 Click on Cell <u>B2</u>, hold down the left mouse button, then drag your mouse down to Cell <u>B5</u> to select the cells.

3 Click on '<u>Format</u>', then '<u>Cells</u>'.

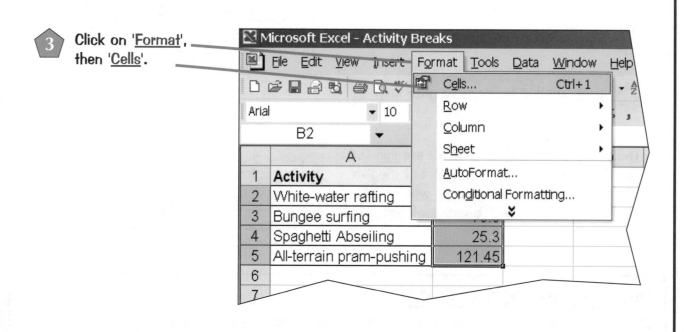

Formatting Numbers

Now Select the Currency Format

4 Click on 'Currency'.

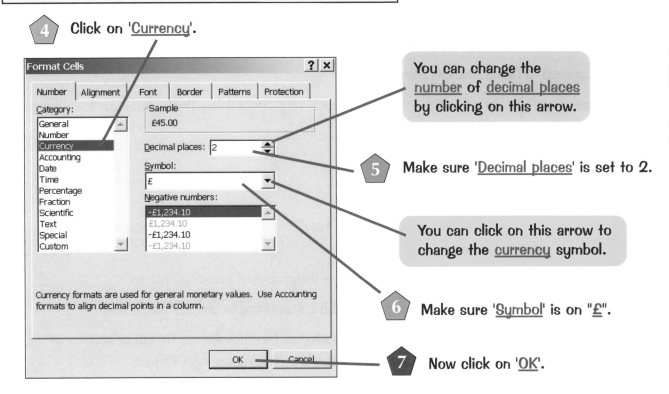

You can change the number of decimal places by clicking on this arrow.

5 Make sure 'Decimal places' is set to 2.

You can click on this arrow to change the currency symbol.

6 Make sure 'Symbol' is on "£".

7 Now click on 'OK'.

The Price Column should look like This

Now your price column has lovely pound signs in front of it, and two decimal places.

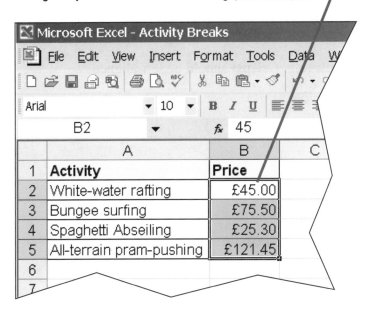

Turning numbers into currency makes you rich (sort of).

But why can't I just type the £ sign in front of it...

If you add a £ sign to the cell, rather than formatting the cells as currency, the spreadsheet may treat the cells as text, not currency, so your formulas won't work. In the assessment, you must format the cells properly, or it'll be marked as an error.

Section Four — Practice Exercises

Keep practising — it's not much further to the end of the book now.

Exercise 1

1.   Open the **Leisure3** spreadsheet.

2.   You need to format the spreadsheet:

   The column heading **Facility** and all row labels (e.g. **Swimming Pool**) should be left-aligned.

   The other column headings should be right-aligned.

   All numeric values should be right-aligned.

3.   Format the data as follows:

   The facility figures for **Jan**, **Feb**, **Mar** and **Total** should be displayed in integer format (to zero decimal places).

   The **Price** figures should be displayed with a £ sign and to 2 decimal places.

   The **Income** figures should be displayed with a £ sign and in integer format.

4.   Enter a formula to calculate the total income for all facilities for the first three months of the year. Make sure this figure is displayed with a £ sign and in integer format.

5.   Save the spreadsheet as **Leisure4**.

Exercise 2

1.   Open the **Tuck Shop2** spreadsheet.

2.   You need to format the spreadsheet:

   The column heading **Item** and all row labels (e.g. **Crisps**) should be left-aligned.

   The other column headings should be right-aligned.

   All numeric values should be right-aligned.

3.   Format the data as follows:

   The sales figures for **Sep**, **Oct**, **Nov** and **Total** should be displayed in integer format (to zero decimal places).

   The **Price** figures should be displayed in integer format.

   The **Income** figures should be displayed with a £ sign and to 2 decimal places.

4.   Insert a new row after **Twix** named **Total Income**.

5.   Enter a formula to calculate the total income for all items sold in the tuck shop.
   Make sure this figure is displayed with a £ and to 2 decimal places.

6.   Save the spreadsheet as **Tuck Shop3**.

Section Four — Practice Exercises

Here's another exercise — you can't have too much practice.

Exercise 3

1. Open the **Agent Sales** spreadsheet.

2. You need to format the spreadsheet:

    The column heading **Agent** and all row labels (e.g. **Hassan**) should be right-aligned.

    The other column headings should be centre-aligned.

    All numeric values should be centre-aligned.

3. Add a new column named **Total** after the **Week 4** column.

    The total for each agent is calculated by adding the figures for **Week 1**, **Week 2**, **Week 3** and **Week 4**.

    Insert a formula to calculate the total for **Hassan**.

    Replicate this formula to show the total for each agent.

4. Insert a new column named **Earnings** before **Base Pay**.

    The earnings for each agent are calculated by multiplying the total sales figures by the rate and adding the base pay.

    Insert a formula to calculate the earnings for **Hassan**.

    Replicate this formula to show the earnings for each agent.

5. Format the data as follows:

    The sales figures for **Week 1**, **Week 2**, **Week 3**, **Week 4** and **Total** should be displayed with a £ sign and in integer format (to zero decimal places).

    The **Base Pay** figures should be displayed in integer format.

    The **Rate** figures should be displayed to 2 decimal places.

    The **Earnings** figures should be displayed with a £ sign and to 2 decimal places.

6. Make sure all numeric values and all column headings (apart from **Agent**) are centre-aligned.

7. Print the spreadsheet with all the formulae showing.

    Make sure that all the formulae are displayed in full.

    Look back to page 17 if you've forgotten how to do this.

8. Save the spreadsheet as **Agent Sales 2**.

Advice for the Assessment

Once you've completed the course, you're ready to take the assessment.
Here's a bit of handy advice to help you out.
You might have heard it before, but read it again — it's useful stuff.

You'll get 2 Hours to Complete the Assessment

You've got plenty of time to do the assessment, so...

- Don't panic.
  - Don't rush — you'll make mistakes.
    - Read the instructions properly, and make sure you follow them.
      - Check your work as you go along, especially your typing.
        - Don't panic. (Did I mention that already?)

Avoid these Errors

If you make a major error, you won't pass. Major errors might include failing to do one of the tasks in the assessment, or having incorrect numeric data or results in your spreadsheet.
So, make sure you follow the instructions carefully.

If you make more than three minor errors, you won't pass the assessment.
So, avoid making small mistakes like these:

1) Making a typing (data entry) error in the text you're asked to enter.

2) Using capital letters in an inconsistent manner.

3) Deleting just the data in a row instead of deleting the row itself.

4) Failing to align data due to an unnecessary space.

5) Changing cells manually (e.g. adding "£" to them), rather than correctly formatting.

6) Saving with the wrong filename.

7) Not typing your name, centre number and the date on your documents.

Watch Out for Data Entry Errors

When you're asked to type something, make sure you type it exactly as it's written,
with the right spacing and punctuation — otherwise you're just throwing easy marks away.

Print your documents to check for errors, then correct
them on the computer before you hand them in.

You need complete inner calm — maybe try yoga...

All the skills you need for Unit 4 are in this book, so as long as you're not tied into some
complicated yoga knot and you've learnt your stuff — you'll have nothing to worry about.

Advice for the Assessment

Here's a checklist you might find handy...

Check that you Know How to Do These Things

<u>Everything</u> you need to know to pass the assessment is in this book.
Use the <u>checklist</u> below to make sure you're <u>confident</u> with all the tasks you could
be asked to do. Go back and look at the <u>relevant pages</u> again if you're not sure.

(Don't tick the boxes unless you're <u>confident</u> you could do the tasks in an <u>exam</u> situation.)

1)	Enter, delete and amend data in spreadsheets.	☐	Pages 10-11
2)	Adjust the size of rows and columns.	☐	Page 12
3)	Add and delete rows and columns.	☐	Page 13
4)	Clear and hide selected cells.	☐	Pages 14-15
5)	Save different versions of spreadsheets.	☐	Page 16
6)	Print spreadsheets showing either data or formulas.	☐	Pages 17
7)	Use simple formulas to add, subtract, multiply and divide.	☐	Pages 20-21
8)	Copy formulas from cell to cell.	☐	Pages 22-23
9)	Use the autosum function.	☐	Page 25
10)	Align data to the left, right or centre of a cell.	☐	Pages 28-29
11)	Format data to a certain number of decimal places.	☐	Pages 30-31
12)	Format data into currency.	☐	Pages 32-33

Smile — there are much
more horrible things you
could be doing.

You're nearly there, keep going...not far now...

If you've ticked all the boxes, you should be ready for a practice assessment.
Try the one over the page to see how you get on.

Section Five — Practice Assessment

Spreadsheets aren't the easiest things to get to grips with, but you're almost finished now. The last thing to do is try this full practice assessment. It's just like the real thing, so it'll give you a really good idea of what you can and can't do. Good luck.

Scenario

You are working as an administrative assistant on the help desk for Lakeland College.

Your manager has asked you to work out the income from the supplies sold at the help desk.

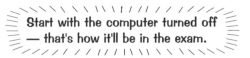

Start with the computer turned off — that's how it'll be in the exam.

1. Switch on the computer and monitor correctly and safely.
   Wait for the operating system software to load fully.

2. Create a new spreadsheet.

3. Enter the following data, leaving the **Total** and **Income** columns blank as shown:

Lakeland College							
Item	Sep	Oct	Nov	Dec	Total	Price	Income
Floppy disks	125	204	68	45		0.2	
CDRs	27	35	12	5		1.99	
Pens	356	240	125	120		0.1	
Pencils	157	280	65	35		0.05	
Paper pads	38	24	26	14		0.99	
Rulers	14	6	8	3		0.5	
Erasers	25	28	6	8		0.1	
Sharpeners	5	8	3	2		0.35	
Correction fluid	26	33	21	24		1.15	
Total income							

4. Enter your name, centre number and today's date a few lines below the data.

5. The total for each item is calculated by adding the figures for **Sep**, **Oct**, **Nov** and **Dec**.

   a) Insert a formula to calculate the total for **Floppy disks**.

   b) Replicate this formula to show the total for each item.

6. Your manager wants you to calculate the income for the items sold at the help desk.

   a) Insert a formula which calculates the **Income** for the **Floppy disks** by multiplying the **Total** by the **Price**.

   b) Replicate this formula to show the **Income** for all the items.

   c) Calculate the **Total income** by adding together all the **Income** figures.
   Insert the formula in the **Income** column on the **Total income** row.

Section Five — Practice Assessment

7. Save your spreadsheet with the filename **helpdesk** and print one copy, showing the figures not the formulae. Make sure that all the data is displayed in full.

8. Your manager has asked you to format the spreadsheet. Apply the following alignment:

   a) The column heading **Item** and all row labels (e.g. **Floppy disks**) should be left-aligned.

   b) All other column headings (e.g. **Sep**, **Oct**) should be right-aligned.

   c) All numeric entries should be right-aligned.

9. Format the data as follows:

   a) The figures for the **Price** column should be displayed with a £ sign to 2 decimal places.

   b) The figures for the **Income** column, including the figure on the **Total income** row, should be displayed with a £ sign and in integer format (to zero decimal places).

10. The manager wants some changes made and errors corrected.

    a) The data for the **Paper pads** is not to be used. Delete this entire row.

    b) The item numbers for January are to be included in the figures.
    Insert a column headed **Jan** between **Dec** and **Total**. The heading **Jan** and the figures should be right-aligned. Enter the **Jan** figures as follows:

Floppy disks	59
CDRs	15
Pens	167
Pencils	89
Rulers	16
Erasers	5
Sharpeners	2
Correction fluid	12

    c) Make sure that the formulae for **Total** and **Income** are updated to include **Jan**.

11. Make the following amendments to the spreadsheet:

    a) The **CDRs** item should be called **Rewriteable CDs**.

    b) The **Price** for **Correction fluid** should be **£2.25**.

    c) The **Erasers** figure for **Nov** should be 18.

12. Save the spreadsheet with the filename **income** and print one copy, showing the figures not the formulae. Make sure that all the data is displayed in full.

13. Print the spreadsheet showing its formulae. Make sure that all formulae are displayed in full.

14. Close the spreadsheet and exit the software securely.

Index

CL4SS1